KARL LANG

ANDALUSIA PANORAMA

Text by Iris Lemanczyk

EDITION**PANORAMA**

ANDALUSIEN

Andalusien ist voller Kontraste. Der ewige Schnee der Sierra Nevada ist gerade mal eine Autostunde von Strand, Palmen und Meer entfernt. Einsame Bergpfade, wo sich Geier und Luchse gute Nacht sagen, liegen nahe bei Hotelburgen und Massentourismus. Uralte knorrige Korkeichenwälder und leuchtend gelbe Sonnenblumenfelder. Hitzeflirrende Wüste und pulverige Skipisten gehören dazu, wie Atlantik und Mittelmeer und das unvergleichliche maurische Erbe: die Alhambra, die trutzige Festungsanlage von Granada, und die Mezquita, die große Moschee von Cordoba. Steinreich und bitterarm sind nur ein paar Schritte voneinander entfernt. Von Huelva im Westen, nach Almeria im Osten, von Gibraltar im Süden, nach Pozoblanco im Norden reicht die südlichste Region Spaniens.

Andalusien lebt von und mit seinen Klischees. Sinnlicher Flamenco, blutiger Stierkampf, trockener Sherry. Und Carmen. Die stolze Arbeiterin in einer Zigarettenfabrik in Sevilla, die der französische Schriftsteller Prosper Mérimée erschaffen hat, gilt als Prototypin einer andalusischen Frau. Sie war Vorlage für Georges Bizets gleichnamige Oper und den Tanzfilm von Carlos Saura. 1840 beklagte sich der Schriftsteller Theophile Gautier, dass die andalusischen Frauen ihm das Lokalkolorit vorenthalten würden, da sie sich nicht wie Carmen kleideten. Außer Carmen gibt es noch das Klischee des Fraueneroberers Don Juan aus Sevilla, den Molière, Goldoni, Lenau, Mozart, Strauss und viele andere zum Helden ihrer Werke machten.

ANDALUSIA

Andalusia is full of contrasts. The eternal snow of the Sierra Nevada is only one hour by car away from the beach, palm trees and sea. Lonely mountain paths where vultures and lynxes hunt lie close to multi-story hotels and mass tourism. Ancient forests of gnarled cork oak and swaying fields of brilliant yellow sunflowers. Arid desert shimmering in the heat haze and powdery ski slopes, stretching from the Atlantic to the Mediterranean, and the incomparable Moorish architecture dating from the Middle Ages: the Alhambra, the defiant fortress of Granada, and the Mezquita, the Great Mosque of Cordoba. Fabulous wealth and bitter poverty can be found in close proximity. This southernmost region of Spain extends from Huelva in the west to Almeria in the east, and from Gibraltar in the south to Pozoblanco in the north.

Andalusia lives from and with its clichés. The sensual flamenco, gory bullfighting and dry sherry. And Carmen – the proud worker in a cigarette factory in Seville, created by the French author Prosper Mérimée, who has come to be regarded as the model of Andalusian women. She became the main character of Georges Bizet's eponymous opera and the dance film by Carlos Saura. In 1840, the author Theophile Gautier complained that the Andalusian women were depriving him of any local colour, since they were not dressed like Carmen. In addition to Carmen there is also the cliché of the great lover Don Juan of Seville, who Molière, Goldoni, Lenau, Mozart, Strauss and many others made the hero of their works.

ANDALOUSIE

L'Andalousie est une terre pleine de contrastes. Les neiges éternelles de la Sierra Nevada sont à une heure de route à peine de la plage, des palmiers et de la mer. Des lynx et des vautours se croisent sur des sentiers de montagne solitaires qui s'étirent à proximité de complexes hôteliers abritant le tourisme de masse. Des forêts séculaires de chênes-lièges noueux contrastent avec le jaune brillant des champs de tournesols. Un désert écrasé sous une chaleur accablante pas loin de pistes de ski sur de la neige poudreuse. Toutes ces choses sont typiques de l'Andalousie au même titre que l'Atlantique et la Méditerranée et bien sûr l'incomparable héritage maure : l'Alhambra, l'orgueilleuse forteresse de Grenade, et la Mezquita, la grande mosquée de Cordoue. Ici, la grande richesse peut côtoyer la grande pauvreté. L'Andalousie, région la plus méridionale d'Espagne, s'étend de Huelva à l'ouest à Almería à l'est, de Gibraltar au sud, à Pozoblanco au nord.
L'Andalousie vit de et avec ses clichés. Le flamenco sensuel, la corrida sanguinaire, le sherry sec. Et bien sûr Carmen. Le personnage de la fière ouvrière d'une usine de cigarettes à Séville créé par l'écrivain français Prosper Mérimée, est considéré comme le prototype de la femme andalouse. Elle est l'héroïne de l'opéra du même nom de Georges Bizet ainsi que du film musical de Carlos Saura. En 1840, l'écrivain Théophile Gautier reproche aux Andalouses de lui cacher la couleur locale, car elles ne s'habillent pas comme Carmen. A côté de ce personnage, il y a bien sûr aussi le

ANDALUCÍA

Andalucía es un mundo de contrastes. La playa, las palmeras y el mar se encuentran a sólo una hora escasa en automóvil de las nieves eternas de la Sierra Nevada. Los linces y los buitres se cruzan en solitarios senderos de montaña que discurren junto a los complejos hoteleros que albergan el turismo de masas. Antiquísimos bosques de nudosos alcornocales forman un pintoresco contraste con el brillante color amarillo de los vecinos campos de girasoles. Aquí se pueden encontrar desiertos que hacen vibrar de calor el aire no lejos de pistas de esquí de nieve en polvo. Todas estas cosas son tan típicas de Andalucía como el Atlántico, el Mediterráneo o su incomparable herencia árabe: La Alhambra, el orgulloso palacio-fortaleza de Granada y la gran Mezquita de Córdoba. En esta región se puede encontrar una riqueza impresionante separada tan sólo por unos pasos de una profunda pobreza. Andalucía, la región más meridional de España se extiende de Huelva en el oeste a Almería en el este y de Gibraltar en el sur a Pozoblanco en el norte.
Andalucía vive con y de sus tópicos. El sensual flamenco, la sangrienta corrida de toros y el jerez seco. Y Carmen. La figura de la orgullosa trabajadora de una fábrica de tabacos de Sevilla que creó el escritor francés Prosper Mérimée y que ha quedado en la mente colectiva como el prototipo de la mujer andaluza. La novela fue el modelo para la ópera del mismo nombre de Georges Bizets y para el musical de Carlos Saura. En 1840 el autor Theophile Gautier se quejaba de que las mujeres andaluzas le ocultaban el colo-

ANDALUSIA

L'Andalusia è una terra di contrasti. Le nevi eterne della Sierra Nevada distano una sola ora dalle spiagge, dalle palme e dal mare. Solitari sentieri di montagna dove avvoltoi e linci si danno la buona notte coesistono con i grandi complessi alberghieri e il turismo di massa. Secolari boschi di nodose querce da sughero e splendenti campi di gialli girasoli. La calura che annebbia la vista all'orizzonte e le piste da sci coperte di neve fine sono opposti che convivono in questo paese come l'Atlantico e il Mediterraneo e l'incomparabile eredità moresca: la fortezza erta a difendere Granada, e la Mezquita, la grande moschea di Cordova. Il confine tra l'opulenza e la misera è sottile. Da Huelva ad Ovest ad Almeria ad Est, da Gibilterra a Sud a Pozoblanco a Nord si estende la regione più meridionale della Spagna.
L'Andalusia vive – e convive – con i suoi luoghi comuni. La sensualità del flamenco, sangue ed arena, lo sherry secco, Carmen. La fiera operaia di una manifattura di tabacchi di Siviglia, creata dalla penna dallo scrittore francese Mérimée, è la donna andalusa per antonomasia, modello per l'opera omonima di Georges Bizet e il film sulla danza di Carlos Saura. Nel 1840 lo scrittore Theophile Gautier lamentava che le donne andaluse, non vestendosi come Carmen, lo privassero di quel particolare tocco di colore locale. Oltre a Carmen sopravvive ancor oggi il mito del rubacuori Don Giovanni da Siviglia, l'eroe celebrato da Molière, Goldoni, Lenau, Mozart, Strauss e molti altri nelle loro opere.

Was Andalusien so faszinierend anders macht sind die Hinterlassenschaften der Araber und Mauren. Elf Jahre benötigten die Araber im vierten Jahrhundert, um Spanien zu unterwerfen. Sie blieben beinahe 800 Jahre. Andalusien hat davon profitiert. Die neuen Herren bauen bisher unbekannte Produkte wie Reis, Pfirsiche, Zuckerrohr, Aprikosen und Baumwolle an. Die Bauern lernen Düngemethoden und raffinierte Bewässerungsanlagen kennen. Viele Einheimische finden Lohn und Brot in Papiermühlen, Webereien und Keramikfabriken. Die Araber richten Bibliotheken ein, die der Volksbildung und nicht der religiösen Beeinflussung dienen. Sie sind in Religionsfragen tolerant, es herrscht Glaubensfreiheit.
Die maurische Herrschaft ab 1248 beschränkt sich auf Granada und Umgebung. Sie zeigt den Andalusiern das Schachspiel und wie man mit Flötentönen becirct. Architektur und Kultur gewinnen. Die Araber bringen ihre symbolhafte Baukunst, ihren Reichtum an Dekorationsformen und das Wunder orientalischer Gärten aus Tausendundeiner Nacht. Al-Andaluz avanciert zur Brücke zwischen Rom und Mekka.
Allem voran die Alhambra. Hoch über der Stadt, die schneebedeckten Gipfel der Sierra Nevada im Rücken, von mächtigen Mauern beschützt, wirkt die Festung wie ein Märchen. Wie die Schalen einer Zwiebel verbergen die verwinkelten Mauern Audienzsäle, Höfe, Moscheen, Bäder und Wohnhäuser. Die Rundbögen und Säulen sind voller Ornamente. Zwölf Löwen aus schwarzem Marmor tragen eine Alabasterschale als Springbrunnen, dessen Wasser in die vier Himmelsrichtungen fließt. 150 Jahre residierten

What makes Andalusia so fascinatingly different are the legacies left behind by the Arabs and Moors. It took the Arabs 11 years before they became masters of Spain from the year 711. They stayed for almost 800 years, and Andalusia has benefited from this fact. The new rulers cultivated previously unknown products such as rice, peaches, sugarcane, apricots and cotton. The farmers were introduced to new methods of fertilisation and sophisticated irrigation systems. Many of the natives found employment and a livelihood in paper mills, weaving mills and ceramics factories. The Arabs established libraries, not for the purposes of religious influence, but for popular education. Moorish rule was restricted from 1248 to Granada and the surrounding area. They introduced to the Andalusians the game of chess and the enchanting notes of the flute. Architecture and culture both benefited. They brought with them their symbolic architectural style, their wealth of decorative design and the wonder of oriental gardens from the "Tales of 1001 Arabian Nights". Al-Andaluz as it was known in Arabic progressed to become a bridge between Rome and Mecca.
Above all stands the Alhambra. Towering high over the city against the background of the snow-covered peaks of the Sierra Nevada, protected by mighty walls, the fortress is like something out of a fairytale. Like the layers of an onion, the angled walls conceal audience chambers, courtyards, mosques, bath-houses and living quarters. The arches and columns are covered in ornament and decoration. Twelve lions sculpted from black marble support an alabaster bowl and fountain, whose water flows out in all four cardinal

stéréotype du bourreau des cœurs, Don Juan de Séville, dont Molière, Goldoni, Lenau, Mozart, Strauss et beaucoup d'autres ont fait le héros de leurs œuvres.

La fascination qu'exerce l'Andalousie sur les touristes est principalement due à son héritage arabe et maure. Il a fallu onze ans aux Arabes avant de régner à partir de 711 sur l'Espagne où ils sont restés presque 800 ans. Cette période a d'ailleurs été bénéfique à l'Andalousie : les nouveaux maîtres cultivent des produits jusqu'ici inconnus comme le riz, les pêches, la canne à sucre, les abricots et le coton. Les paysans découvrent de nouvelles méthodes d'amendement des sols ainsi que des systèmes d'irrigation raffinés. De nombreux habitants trouvent du travail dans les moulins à papier, les ateliers de tissage et les usines de céramique. Les Arabes créent des bibliothèques destinées à instruire le peuple et non à servir d'instrument d'asservissement religieux.

La domination maure à partir de 1248 se limite à Grenade et ses environs. Grâce à elle, les Andalous apprennent les échecs ainsi que l'art de jouer de la flûte. L'architecture et la culture profitent de cette influence arabe, de son style symbolique, de la richesse de ses formes décoratives et de la magie des jardins orientaux des Mille et une Nuits. Al-Andalus est désormais un pont jeté entre Rome et La Mecque. Et dominant le tout, l'Alhambra. Loin au-dessus de la ville, avec les sommets enneigés de la Sierra Nevada pour toile de fond et protégée par d'imposantes murailles, cette forteresse semble sortir tout droit d'un conte de fées. Dans son enceinte, d'innombrables murs sinueux disposés comme les peaux d'un oignon dissimulent salles d'audience, cours,

rido local, de que no se vestían como “Carmen”. Además del de Carmen también existe el estereotipo del conquistador Don Juan de Sevilla, el héroe de tantas obras de Molière, Goldoni, Lenau, Mozart, Strauss y muchos otros.

Lo que hace a Andalucía tan fascinantemente diferente son las huellas del pasado árabe y bereber. Once años necesitaron los árabes para consumar su dominio de España a partir de 711. Su presencia duró casi 800 años. Andalucía se benefició de su dominio. Los nuevos dominadores trajeron productos desconocidos en aquel momento como el arroz, los melocotones, la caña de azúcar, los albaricoques y el algodón. Los campesinos aprendieron métodos de abono y cómo construir refinadas instalaciones de regadío. Muchos de los habitantes nativos encontraron trabajo en los molinos de papel, en las tejedurías y en las fábricas de cerámica. Los árabes establecieron bibliotecas que tenían como objetivo la educación popular y no la expansión religiosa.

A partir de 1248 la zona de dominio musulmán queda reducida a Granada y su entorno. A través del reino de Granada llegaron a los andaluces el ajedrez y el arte de tocar la flauta. Además la arquitectura y la cultura de este reino de taifas alcanzaron a partir de esa fecha el apogeo de su fuerza simbólica y de su riqueza de formas decorativas así como el milagroso encanto de los jardines orientales de Granada, que parecen extraídos de los cuentos de las mil y una noches. Al-Andalus se convirtió en un puente de conexión entre Roma y la Meca.

Y dominándolo todo está la Alhambra. En lo más alto de la ciudad, ante el impresionante panorama de las cimas cubiertas de nieve de Sierra Nevada que le sirve de fondo y

L'Andalusia deve il suo fascino così particolare all'eredità araba e moresca. Undici anni resistette la Spagna prima di arrendersi alla conquista araba, iniziata nel 711. Gli arabi vi rimasero in seguito per quasi 800 anni e l'Andalusia beneficiò della loro presenza nel suo territorio. I nuovi conquistatori piantarono prodotti sconosciuti fino all'epoca come il riso, le pesche, la canna da zucchero, le albicocche e il cotone. I contadini appresero metodi di concimazione e iniziarono ad utilizzare sofisticati impianti d'irrigazione. Molte popolazioni locali trovarono fonte di lavoro e sostentamento nei mulini da carta, le tessiture e le botteghe per la produzione della ceramica. Gli arabi aprirono biblioteche per diffondere la conoscenza tra la gente che non fu strumentalizzata a fini religiosi.

La dominazione araba, iniziata nel 1248, restò circoscritta alla città di Granada e alle aree limitrofe. Gli andalusi impararono a giocare a scacchi e a eseguire maliose melodie con il flauto. L'architettura e la cultura si arricchirono dei nuovi apporti provenienti da quell'arte e dal suo simbolismo figurativo, dalla ricchezza delle decorazioni e dalla meraviglia dei giardini orientali delle Mille e Una Notte. Al-Andaluz divenne così un ponte ideale tra Roma e La Mecca, soprattutto attraverso l'Alhambra. Sovrastante la città, la vetta innevata della Sierra Nevada sullo sfondo, protetta da imponenti mura, la fortezza si staglia nel suo fascino fiabesco. Come scatole cinesi le mura tortuose nascondono sale d'udienza, cortili, moschee, bagni e abitazioni. Gli archi a tutto sesto e le colonne sono finemente decorate. Dodici leoni in marmo nero sorreggono un bacile in alabastro, una fontana la cui acqua zampilla

die maurischen Könige dort, bevor 1492 der letzte muslimische Herrscher Muhammed XI. vor dem katholischen Königspaar Ferdinand von Aragon und Isabella von Kastillien kapitulierte. Um einen runden Innenhof ließ sich Kaiser Karl V. einen Palast in die Anlage hineinbauen.
„Hätte ich gewusst, was Ihr vorhabt, wärt Ihr nicht dazu gekommen, es durchzuführen. Das, was Ihr hier hinstellt, bekommt man an jeder Straßenecke zu sehen, aber das, was hier einmal war, hat es auf der ganzen Welt nur einmal gegeben." Mit diesen Worten tadelte Karl V. die Dombauherren, die 1523 eine christliche Kathedrale in die Moschee von Cordoba setzten. Zweihundert Jahre dauerte die Bauzeit der Moschee. 785 wurde im Auftrag von Abd Ar Rahman I. damit begonnen, damals war Cordoba ein selbstständiges Emirat sowie geistiges und kulturelles Zentrum des Islam. Trotz der langen Bauzeit strahlt die Mezquita Einheitlichkeit aus. Neunzehn Schiffe erstrecken sich von Nord nach Süd, sie sind durch 856 Säulen getrennt. Ein steinener Wald voller Säulen. Mit weiß-gelben und rostroten Keilsteinen. Im Dämmerlicht der Moschee entsteht dadurch ein scheinbar grenzenloses Labyrinth. Höhepunkt maurischer Baukunst.
Ein ganz anderes Fest für Ästheten, aber auch noch von maurischer Architektur beeinflusst, sind Andalusiens weiße Dörfer. Pueblo Blanco. Wie Schneefelder bedecken die weiß gekalkten Dörfer die Hügel und Berge im Südwesten. Eng. Verschachtelt. Schutz vor Hitze und Kälte bietend. Von Bögen überspannt. Blumengeschmückt. Weißer Kalk wird großzügig verwendet. Ein Weiß, das sich mit keinem anderen vergleichen lässt. Ein Weiß, das in den Augen

points of the compass. The Moorish kings resided here for 150 years, before the last Muslim ruler Muhammed XI capitulated to the Catholic royal couple Ferdinand of Aragon and Isabella of Castile in 1492. King Charles V had a palace built within the complex around a circular inner courtyard.
"Had I known what you intended, you would not have had the chance to do it. What you have built here can be seen on every street corner, but what used to be here was unique throughout the world." These were the words with which Charles V reprimanded the cathedral builders who in 1523 inserted an entire Christian chapel inside the Mosque of Cordoba. The mosque was originally built over a period of 200 years. Construction started in 785 at the direction of Abd Ar Rahman I, at which time Cordoba was an independent emirate and spiritual and cultural centre of Islam. Despite the long construction period, the Mezquita radiates uniformity. 19 aisles extend from north to south, separated from each other by 856 columns. A petrified forest of stone columns, with arch bricks of whitish yellow and rust red. In the cool twilight of the mosque, this creates an apparently boundless labyrinth, and represents the zenith of Moorish architecture.
Quite a different feast for aesthetes, but still greatly influenced by Moorish architecture, are Andalusia's shimmering white villages, the "pueblos blancos". In the southwest of the region, the whitewashed villages cover the hills and mountains like fields of snow. Tightly-packed, shoulder-to-shoulder, the houses offer protection against both heat and cold. Spanned by arches and decorated with flower boxes, white

mosquées, bains et résidences. Les arcs en plein cintre et les colonnes sont couverts d'un foisonnement d'ornements. Douze lions de marbre noir portent la vasque en albâtre d'une fontaine dont les jets sont dirigés vers les quatre points cardinaux. Les rois maures résident ici 150 ans jusqu'à la capitulation, en 1492, du dernier seigneur musulman, Mohamed XI, devant le couple royal catholique Ferdinand d'Aragon et Isabelle de Castille. Leur successeur, l'empereur Charles Quint, fait construire un palais autour d'une cour intérieure ronde dans l'enceinte de l'Alhambra. «Si j'avais su ce qu'il y avait ici, je n'aurais jamais osé toucher à l'ancien édifice. Vous avez détruit quelque chose d'unique au monde, et avez construit ce que l'on voit partout». C'est en ces termes que Charles Quint blâme les architectes qui, en 1523, édifient une cathédrale chrétienne au milieu de la mosquée de Cordoue. Les travaux de construction de la mosquée ont duré deux siècles alors qu'ils avaient commencé en 785 sur l'ordre d'Abd Ar Rahman Ier, à l'époque où Cordoue était un émirat indépendant ainsi qu'un centre spirituel et culturel de l'Islam. En dépit de la durée des travaux, la Mezquita est un ouvrage homogène avec dix-neuf nefs du nord au sud, séparées par 856 colonnes. Une véritable forêt de colonnes en pierre avec des voussoirs blanc-jaune et rouille. Dans la pénombre de la mosquée, on a l'impression de se trouver dans un labyrinthe apparemment sans fin. Probablement le fleuron de l'architecture maure.

Les esthètes ne manqueront pas non plus les villages blancs d'Andalousie, clairement influencés par l'architecture maure. Pueblo Blanco. Ces villages aux maisons blanchies

custodiado por poderosas murallas, el palacio-fortaleza parece sacado de una leyenda. Los arcos curvados y las columnas están cubiertos de ornamentos. Doce leones de mármol negro portan el cuenco de alabastro de una fuente saltarina cuyas aguas fluyen hacia los cuatro puntos cardinales. Aquí residieron los reyes moros durante 150 años, hasta 1492; el año de la capitulación de Muhammed XI, el último soberano musulmán, ante los reyes católicos, Fernando de Aragón e Isabel de Castilla. Posteriormente el emperador Carlos V se hizo construir un palacio en torno a un patio redondo en el interior del recinto de la Alhambra.

"Si hubiera sabido lo que os proponíais, no lo hubierais podido hacer. Lo que habéis colocado aquí, se puede ver en cualquier esquina, pero lo que antes había aquí era único en todo el mundo". Con estas palabras reprochó Carlos V su acción a los constructores que en 1523 edificaron una catedral cristiana en medio de la Mezquita de Córdoba. La construcción de la mezquita duró doscientos años y comenzó en 785 por encargo de Abd Ar Rahman I. En aquel entonces Córdoba ya era un emirato independiente así como uno de los centros culturales y religiosos del Islam. A pesar del largo período de construcción, la mezquita muestra un aspecto uniforme. Alberga diecinueve naves que se extienden de norte a sur divididas por 856 columnas. Todo un bosque pétreo de columnas adornadas de dovelas blancoamarillas y rojizas. En la penumbra de la mezquita las columnas parecen formar un laberinto sin límites. Sin duda el auge del arte constructivo árabe.

Otro placer muy diferente para los estetas son los pueblos blancos de Andalucía que también muestran una clara in-

nei quattro punti cardinali. I re moreschi abitarono questa residenza per 150 anni prima che, nel 1492, l'ultimo sovrano musulmano Mohamed XI capitolasse a favore della coppia reale cattolica di Ferdinando d'Aragona e Isabella di Castiglia. L'imperatore Carlo V si fece costruire nel complesso un palazzo attorno ad un cortile interno circolare.

„Avessi saputo le vostre intenzioni non sareste riusciti a realizzarle. Quello che avete qui costruito lo si può vedere all'angolo di qualsiasi strada. Quello che invece sorgeva prima era un'opera unica al mondo." Con queste parole Carlo V riproverò i costruttori del duomo che nel 1523 realizzarono una cattedrale cristiana sulla moschea di Cordova, la cui costruzione durò duecento anni. I lavori ebbero inizio nel 785 per ordine di Abd Ar Rahman I. All'epoca Cordova era un emirato indipendente ed un centro spirituale e culturale dell'Islam. Nonostante la sua costruzione avesse richiesto un tempo così lungo, la Mezquita trasmette un'impressione di coerenza stilistica. Diciannove navate si estendono da nord a sud, divise da 856 colonne. Una foresta di colonne di pietra, con mattoni a cuneo bianco-gialli e rosso ruggine. Nella penombra della moschea le linee e i colori compongono l'immagine di un labirinto apparentemente infinito. Il trionfo dell'architettura moresca.

Altrettanta raffinatezza, anch'essa influenzata dall'architettura moresca, contraddistingue i villaggi bianchi andalusi, (Pueblo Blanco). Come coltri di neve i villaggi imbiancati a calce coprono le colline e le montagne del sudovest. Stretti. Intricati. Riparati dalla calura e dal freddo. Coper-

brennt. Der Kalk wirkt nicht nur desinfizierend, sondern reflektiert auch die Sonnenstrahlen. Dadurch bleibt es in den Häusern angenehm temperiert. Die Abendsonne bringt das Weiß zu einem fast überirdischen Leuchten. Nicht selten liegen in den Dörfern christliche Kirchen neben arabischen Kastellen. Gegensatz und Gemeinsamkeit zweier großer Kulturen. Gegensätze wie Tag und Nacht. Nachts erwacht der Himmel in den Bergen. Wahre Lichtprozessionen ziehen dann über das Firmament. Die Verstorbenen, die als Sterne auferstehen, wandern durch die Nacht, glaubt man hier oben.

Die Sierra Nevada, das Schneegebirge, ist das zweithöchste Gebirge Europas. Sierra, das spanische Wort für Gebirge, bedeutet wörtlich Säge. Ein passender Name für die schroffen und kargen Berge. Bis ins 20. Jahrhundert drangen nur die Neveros, die Eismänner, die ihre Eisblöcke im nahen Granada verkauften, dorthin. Jahrelang waren die Berge lediglich Kulisse für die Alhambra. Aber in den vergangenen Jahrzehnten ist die Sierra Nevada immer populärer geworden – zum Wandern, Skilaufen, Klettern und Mountainbiken. Trotzdem finden hier noch Geier, die über hitzeflirrenden Felswänden kreisen, ein ungestörtes Refugium, genauso wie Steinböcke und Bergziegen. Uralte Steineichen werfen ihre Schatten. Üppige Wildblumenwiesen gedeihen in den Hochtälern. Trotz Hirten, Hirschen und Hitze ist Platz für Einsamkeit und Abenteuer.

Davon ist an der Costa del Sol nichts zu merken. Massentourismus bei 300 Sonnentagen im Jahr. Torremolinos. Eine endlose Reihe gesichtsloser grauer Hotelblocks, die bis zu 15 Stockwerke hoch gewachsen sind. Seit 1957 das

chalk is used liberally. A white that cannot be compared with any other. A white that seems to burn into the eyes. The chalk not only looks antiseptically clean, but also reflects the sunlight, leaving the houses pleasantly cool. The evening sunlight gives the white an almost unearthly luminescence. In many villages, Christian churches stand side-by-side with Arabic forts. The contrast and common ground of two great cultures. Contrasts like day and night. At night, the sky in the mountains comes alive, and processions of light march across the firmament. The people up here believe that these are the dead, who rise again as stars to wander the night.

The Sierra Nevada, the snowy mountains, is the second-highest mountain chain in Europe. Sierra, the Spanish word for mountain, literally means "saw" – an appropriate name for the craggy and barren peaks. As late as the 20th Century, the only people to be seen here were the "neveros", the icemen, who cut blocks of ice here to sell in nearby Granada. For years the mountains were nothing more than the background setting for the Alhambra. Over recent decades however, the Sierra Nevada has become increasingly popular – for rambling, skiing, climbing and mountain-biking. Nevertheless vultures can still be found here in this undisturbed haven, circling in the shimmering thermals thrown up by the sheer rock walls, together with ibex and mountain goats. Ancient holly oaks still cast their shadows. Luxurious meadows of wildflowers flourish in the upland valleys. Despite the shepherds, deer and the heat, there is still plenty of room for loneliness and adventure.

There is nothing of this however on the Costa del Sol. Mass tourism with 300 days of sun per year. Torremolinos – an

à la chaux coiffent les collines et les montagnes dans le sud-ouest comme des champs de neige. Avec leurs ruelles étroites et tortueuses, ils offrent un abri idéal contre la chaleur et le froid. Des villages généreusement blanchis à la chaux décorés d'arcs et de fleurs. Des villages d'une blancheur incomparable. Une blancheur qui brûle les yeux car la chaux non seulement désinfecte mais elle reflète aussi les rayons du soleil, grâce à quoi la température reste agréablement tempérée à l'intérieur des maisons. Le soleil couchant sublime la clarté des murs, la rendant presque surnaturelle. Il n'est pas rare, dans ces villages, qu'une église chrétienne jouxte un castel arabe, soulignant les antagonismes et les points communs de deux grandes cultures. Des contrastes comme le jour et la nuit. La nuit, le ciel s'éveille au-dessus des montagnes et de véritables processions de lumières parcourent alors le firmament. On croit ici que ce sont les défunts, renaissant sous forme d'étoiles, qui errent à travers la nuit.

La Sierra Nevada, montagne enneigée, est le deuxième plus haut massif d'Europe. Sierra qui veut dire en espagnol montagne, signifie littéralement scie. Un nom parfaitement approprié pour désigner ces montagnes escarpées et arides. Jusqu'au 20ème siècle, seuls les « neveros » s'y aventurent pour en ramener des blocs de glace qu'ils vendent ensuite dans la ville proche de Grenade. Pendant des années, la Sierra Nevada s'est contentée de servir de décor à l'Alhambra, mais elle connaît un regain de popularité depuis plusieurs décennies – auprès des amateurs de randonnée, de ski, d'escalade et de VTT. Heureusement, les vautours qui décrivent des cercles au-dessus des parois rocheuses écrasées de chaleur

fluencia árabe. Estos pueblos encalados cubren como campos de nieve las colinas y las montañas de la Andalucía suroccidental. Pueblos de calles estrechas y enrevesadas que ofrecen un refugio ideal contra el calor y el frío. Pueblos de muros generosamente cubiertos de cal y decorados con arcos y flores. Pueblos de una blancura tal, que resulta incomparable. De un color blanco que refulge y quema en los ojos, pues la cal no sólo tiene la ventaja de ser desinfectante, sino que también refleja los rayos del sol. De esta forma se logra que las casas mantengan una agradable temperatura. El sol de la tarde sublima la claridad de los muros hasta convertirla en una luminosidad casi sobrenatural. A menudo la iglesia cristiana de estos pueblos se encuentra junto al castillo moro subrayando así la antítesis y los puntos en común de dos grandes culturas. Contrastes como el de la noche y el del día. Por las noches el cielo parece despertar sobre las montañas. Es entonces cuando en el firmamento se dibujan verdaderas procesiones de luminarias. Aquí se cree que los difuntos, que renacen como estrellas, vagan a través de la noche.

Sierra Nevada es la segunda sierra más alta de Europa. La palabra española sierra, que también denomina la herramienta cortante, resulta apropiadísima para estas escarpadas y áridas montañas. Hasta el siglo XX sólo se adentraban allí los neveros, los vendedores de bloques de hielo de Granada. Aunque durante muchos años las montañas parecían tener la única función de servir de escenario a la Alhambra, en las últimas décadas la Sierra Nevada ha ido ganando popularidad entre los senderistas, los esquiadores, los montañeros y los ciclistas de montaña. Afortunadamente, y a

ti d'archi. Adorni di fiori. Calce bianca utilizzata in abbondanza. Un bianco assoluto. Un bianco che brucia gli occhi. Oltre ad avere proprietà disinfettanti la calce riflette i raggi del sole: un espediente per mantenere all'interno delle case una temperatura gradevolmente mite. Nelle ore serali il sole trasfigura quel bianco in una luce abbacinante, quasi soprannaturale. Nei villaggi non è raro trovare chiese cristiane costruite in prossimità di un castello arabo. Contrasti e armonie tra due grandi culture. Opposti come il giorno e la notte. Alla notte il cielo si risveglia tra le montagne, mentre vere processioni di luce scorrono nel firmamento. I morti risorgono come stelle per vagare nella notte, secondo una leggenda diffusa tra queste alture.

La Sierra Nevada, la montagna innevata, è la seconda vetta più alta in Europa. Sierra, il termine spagnolo che significa montagna, letteralmente significa sega. Una definizione perfetta per indicare quei monti nudi e scoscesi, in cui fino al XX° secolo s'inerpicavano soltanto i Neveros, i mercanti di neve, per trovare blocchi di ghiaccio da vendere nella vicina Granada. Per molto tempo queste montagne fecero solo da sfondo all'Alhambra. Negli ultimi decenni la Sierra Nevada è invece stata sempre più apprezzata come meta d'escursionisti, sciatori, scalatori e appassionati di mountain bike. Eppure gli avvoltoi che disegnano in volo i loro cerchi dall'alto delle pareti delle rocce arroventate dal sole vi trovano ancora rifugi indisturbati. Anche stambecchi e capre di montagna abitano questi dirupi da cui i lecci secolari proiettano la loro ombra. Prati rigogliosi coperti di fiori selvatici crescono nelle alte valli, luoghi di solitudine e d'avventura nonostante i caprai, i cervi e il caldo cocente.

erste Charterflugzeug bei Torremolinos landete, hat der Hunger der Nord- und Mitteleuropäer nach andalusischer Sonne fast nur zugenommen. Der Massentourismus entfaltete sich unter General Franco, der bis 1975 regierte. Spaniens Diktator wollte aus armen Fischerdörfern das Florida Europas machen. Er verwirklichte seinen Traum mit Geldern aus den USA, die im Gegenzug das Recht erhielten, in Spanien Atomwaffenbasen zu errichten. Sowohl der Jet-Set-Glamour Marbellas, als auch die billigen Pauschalangebote waren ein Riesenerfolg. Auf Kosten von Schönheit und Umwelt der Region.

Für viele Urlauber steht Sevilla auf dem Besuchsprogramm. „Herkules erbaute mich. Julius Caesar umgab mich mit Mauern und Türmen und der Heilige König nahm mich ein", so lautet die Inschrift über einem der Stadttore. Sevilla trägt viele Namen: Tor des Südens, Stadt zwischen Orient und Okzident, Hort der Kastagnetten. Was für ein atemberaubender Anblick am späten Abend! Wenn von den Ufern des Guadalquivir in der Ferne die Silhouette der Stadt mit ihren Türmen, Brücken, Kathedralen und Palästen ihre Schatten wirft. Der träge vorbeiziehende Fluss gehört zu Sevilla wie das abendliche Gewimmel in den Gassen, wie die Plätze mit den kickenden Kindern, wie der Duft von Jasmin und wie Tertulia. Das abendliche Schwätzchen auf Häusertreppen und Gehwegen, bei denen sich die Nachbarn theatralisch und gestenreich erzählen, was sie aufregt, verblüfft, amüsiert oder wie die letzte Semana Santa verlief.

Überall in Andalusien finden in der Semana Santa, der Karwoche, traditionelle Prozessionen statt. Überlebensgroße Figuren des Heilands und der Jungfrau Maria wer-

endless line of faceless grey hotel blocks, rising up to 15 stories in height. Since the first charter aircraft landed at Torremolinos in 1957, the hunger of north and central Europeans for the Andalusian sun has increased almost year by year. Mass tourism developed under General Franco, who governed the country until 1975. Spain's dictator wanted to turn poor fishing villages into the Florida of Europe. He realised his dream with funds from the USA, which in return was granted the right to establish atomic weapons bases in Spain. Both the jet-set glamour of Marbella and the low-cost package tours proved to be an enormous success, although at no small cost to the beauty and environment of the region.

For many holiday-makers, Seville is an essential tour destination. "Hercules built me. Julius Caesar surrounded me with walls and towers and the Holy King took me in", so runs the inscription above one of the city gates. Seville has many names: Gateway to the south, the City between the Orient and Occident, the stronghold of the castanets. What a breathtaking sight awaits the visitor in the late evening, when from the banks of the Guadalquivir the silhouette of the city, with its towers, bridges, cathedrals and palaces, casts its shadow in the distance! The sluggishly flowing river is just as much part of Seville as the evening throng in the narrow streets, the squares full of children playing football, the scent of jasmine and the "tertulia" (a social gathering with literary or artistic overtones). The evening gossip on the house steps and pavements, when neighbours recount to each other with much theatrical gesturing, what excites, astounds or amuses them, or how the last "Semana Santa" went.

ont trouvé ici, en dépit du tourisme, un refuge paisible, tout comme les bouquetins et les chèvres des montagnes. Des chênes-rouvres séculaires projettent leur ombre depuis des temps immémoriaux tandis que dans les vallées de montagne, les prairies sont couvertes de fleurs sauvages. Malgré les bergers, les cerfs et la chaleur, le paysage est assez vaste pour y trouver la solitude et l'aventure.

Ce n'est pas le cas sur la Costa del Sol où domine le tourisme de masse favorisé par 300 journées de soleil par an. Torremolinos : une file interminable d'hôtels gris et anonymes pouvant avoir jusqu'à quinze étages alignés les uns à côté des autres. Depuis 1957, date à laquelle le premier avion charter a atterri près de Torremolinos, le nombre de touristes affamés de soleil andalou en provenance de l'Europe du Nord et de l'Europe Centrale n'a cessé d'augmenter. Le tourisme de masse a connu un véritable essor sous le Général Franco qui a gouverné le pays jusqu'en 1975. Le dictateur espagnol qui voulait faire de villages de pêcheurs une Floride européenne, a pu réaliser son rêve grâce à l'argent des Etats-Unis obtenu en échange de l'implantation de bases atomiques en Espagne. Le glamour de la Jet-Set de Marbella tout comme les voyages organisés bon marché se sont révélés un immense succès, mais cela s'est fait au détriment de la beauté et de l'environnement de la région.

Partout en Andalousie, la Semana Santa, à Pâques, est l'occasion de processions traditionnelles. Des effigies plus grandes que nature du Christ et de la Vierge Marie sont portées à pas mesurés, le paso, à travers la foule recueillie. Les pénitents portant des bougies et des capuchons pointus qui dissimulent leurs traits conduisent les processions.

pesar del turismo, todavía encuentran aquí su último refugio, al igual que las cabras montesas, esos buitres que trazan lentamente sus círculos aéreos sobre paredes de piedra centelleantes de calor mientras que antiquísimas encinas siguen proyectando sus sombras desde tiempos inmemoriales. En los valles de montaña en los que crecen frondosas praderas de flores silvestres el paisaje invita a disfrutar de la soledad y de la aventura a pesar del calor y de la esporádica presencia de pastores y de ciervos.

De ese ambiente no queda nada en la Costa del Sol. Allí domina el turismo de masas 300 días de sol al año. Torremolinos. Una interminable línea de grises bloques de hoteles de hasta 15 plantas que parecen sacados del mismo molde. Desde que en 1957 aterrizó el primer vuelo chárter junto a Torremolinos, el ansia de los noreuropeos y centroeuropeos por disfrutar del sol andaluz ha ido aumentando permanentemente. El turismo de masas se desarrolló bajo el régimen del General Franco, que gobernó hasta 1975. El dictador de España, que quería transformar los pobres pueblos de pescadores en la Florida de Europa, pudo convertir en realidad su sueño con capital procedente de los EE.UU. que, como contrapartida, obtuvieron el derecho de establecer bases atómicas en España. Tanto el establecimiento del ambiente de la "Jet-Set" en Marbella como las ofertas de viajes organizados baratos se convirtieron en un tremendo éxito que se alcanzó en detrimento de la belleza y del medio ambiente de la región.

Por toda Andalucía se celebran las tradicionales procesiones de la Semana Santa. Los pasos con las sagradas imágenes del Salvador y de María son ceremoniosamente

Ben altro è la Costa del Sol. Turismo di massa nei 300 giorni di sole all'anno. Torremolinos. Una linea ininterrotta di anonime costruzioni d'alberghi grigi alte fino a 15 piani. Da quando nel 1957 il primo volo charter atterrò a Torremolinos, la fame di sole andaluso degli abitanti dell'Europa Settentrionale e Centrale è quasi sempre solo aumentata. Il turismo di massa prese piede durante il governo del Generale Franco, che diresse il paese fino al 1975. Il dittatore spagnolo voleva fare di quei poveri villaggi di pescatori la Florida europea. Franco realizzò il suo sogno con fondi statunitensi, che in cambio furono autorizzati a costruire le loro basi militari atomiche in Spagna. Fu così un successo clamoroso sia del jet-set-glamour di Marbella e come dei pacchetti viaggio all-inclusive e il turismo decretò la distruzione della bellezza e delle risorse naturalistiche della regione.

Per molte persone in vacanza in questa zona Siviglia è una tappa obbligata. „Ercole mi costruì. Giulio Cesare mi cinse di mura e torri e il Sacro Re mi accolse " recita l'iscrizione posta in alto su uno dei portali della città. Siviglia ha molte definizioni: porta del sud, città tra oriente ed occidente, patria delle castagnette. Che emozioni regala la città alla sera tardi quando dalle rive del Guadalquivir il profilo della città in lontananza con le sue torri, i ponti, le cattedrali e i palazzi avvolge tutto nelle sue ombre. Il corso indolente del fiume appartiene a Siviglia come il trambusto serale tra i vicoli, i bambini che giocano a pallone delle piazze, il profumo del gelsomino e della tertulia. Le chiacchiere serali sulle scale di casa e i marciapiedi in cui i vicini raccontano con enfasi e ampi gesti le preoccupazioni,

den gemessenen Schrittes, de Paso, durch die andächtige Menge getragen. Büßer mit Kerzen und spitzen Kapuzen, die das Gesicht verhüllen führen die Prozessionen an. In der Kirche segnen sie die von lieblichem Schmerz gezeichnete Madonna.

Und plötzlich ist er zu hören, dieser klare, Schweigen gebietende, sich dehnende und überstürzende Ton. Ein Mann singt die einfache, aber unendliche Qual ausdrückende Melodie, ein Saeta. Es erinnert an die Sänger des Flamenco.

Das Lied braucht sein Publikum. Der Flamenco will nicht gefallen, sondern die Seele aufschließen. Ein Spruch besagt: „Du kannst den Flamenco nicht planen, nicht zwingen. Er ist wie eine Sternschnuppe, manchmal wie ein Blitz, dann zerreißt er dir das Herz." Trotzdem schießen immer mehr Flamenco-Schulen aus dem Boden. Hinter dem Stakkato der Stiefelabsätze verstecken sich Wut und Stolz, die Handbewegungen drücken Zärtlichkeit aus. Der Tocador lässt seine Fingerspitzen über die Gitarrensaiten fliegen. Längst sind die Zuhörer eins geworden mit dem Rhythmus.

Seinem ganz eigenen Rhythmus zwischen Mensch und Tier gehorcht die umstrittene Bastion Andalusien: der Stierkampf. In Andalusien steht seine Wiege. Zu Pasodoble-Klängen ziehen die geschmückten Toreros in die Arena ein. Ernest Hemingway beschreibt in „Tod am Nachmittag" die Angst und Achtung des Toreros vor dem 500 Kilo schweren Tier, aber auch die spielerische Leichtigkeit des rituellen Tötungsaktes. Intelligenz und Geschicklichkeit des Menschen müssen über die Brachialgewalt des Stieres siegen. So will es die uralte Regel des Stierkampfes.

During the Semana Santa or Holy Week, traditional processions are held throughout Andalusia. Larger-than-life effigies of the Saviour and the Virgin Mary are carried "de paso" – slowly and solemnly – past the devout spectators. The processions are led by penitents carrying candles and wearing pointed caps which conceal their face. In the Church, they bless the physical pain of the Madonna.

And suddenly it can be heard, this clear, spreading and onrushing sound that bids all else silence. A man sings the simple but unending melody of the Saeta, reminiscent of the singers of the flamenco, but which nevertheless expresses eternal anguish.

The song needs an audience. The flamenco is not intended to please, but to unlock the soul. One saying runs: "You cannot plan the flamenco, nor force it. It is like a shooting star, or sometimes a bolt of lightning, which then breaks your heart." Nevertheless, or perhaps for this very reason, more and more flamenco schools are springing up. The staccato of the heel-tapping represents anger and pride, while the hand movements express tenderness. The fingertips of the "tocador" flit across the guitar strings. The listeners have long since become one with the rhythm.

In its bastion of Andalusia, the much-disputed "sport" of bullfighting follows its own particular rhythm between man and beast. Bullfighting originated in Andalusia. In their luxurious, embroidered costumes, the toreros enter the arena to the sound of the "paso doble". In his book "Death in the Afternoon", Ernest Hemingway describes the fear and respect of the torero for the 1,000 lb bull, and also the theatrical lightness of the ritual slaughter. The intelligence

Dans l'église, ils bénissent la Vierge qui porte toute la souffrance du monde.
Et soudain, un chant de plus en plus clair, de plus en plus fort, implorant le silence, retentit. Un homme chante une mélodie simple mais exprimant une douleur infinie, une saeta, qui rappelle les chanteurs de flamenco.
Il s'agit d'un type de chant qui a besoin d'un public. Le flamenco ne cherche pas à plaire mais plutôt à toucher l'âme de ceux qui l'écoutent. Un dicton populaire dit : « Tu ne peux pas prévoir le flamenco, le forcer. C'est comme une étoile filante, parfois comme un éclair, qui te déchire le cœur. » Les écoles de flamenco pourtant jaillissent du sol comme des champignons. Derrière le staccato des talons de bottes, se cachent la colère et la fierté d'un peuple, tandis que la gestuelle des mains exprime sa tendresse. Le tocador fait voltiger le bout de ses doigts sur les cordes de sa guitare, les auditeurs et le rythme ne font qu'un depuis longtemps.
Le bastion le plus controversé de l'Andalousie, la corrida, obéit à son propre rythme entre l'homme et l'animal. L'Andalousie est le berceau de la tauromachie. Les toreros, parés d'un magnifique habit de lumière, font leur entrée dans l'arène aux sons du pasodoble. Ernest Hemingway décrit dans son livre « Mort dans l'après-midi » la peur et le respect des toreros face à l'animal de 500 kilos, mais aussi la légèreté ludique de la mise à mort rituelle. L'intelligence et l'adresse de l'homme doivent vaincre la force brutale du taureau, comme l'exige la tradition séculaire de la corrida.
Des durs d'un tout autre genre travaillent dans le seul et unique désert naturel d'Europe, le désert d'Almería, carac-

portados a hombros a través de las emocionadas muchedumbres. Los nazarenos con sus velas y sus caperuzas que ocultan el rostro son las figuras centrales de las procesiones. En las iglesias se bendice la sagrada imagen de la Virgen Dolorosa.
Y de pronto se percibe apenas en el ambiente un canto que va cobrando fuerza y claridad mientras invita al silencio. Un hombre se ha lanzado a cantar una saeta, esa expresión melodiosa de la profunda pena por Cristo. La saeta recuerda a los cantantes de flamenco.
Se trata de un tipo de copla que vive de su público, ya que el cante flamenco no pretende agradar, sino tocar el alma de los oyentes. Un dicho popular lo expresa así: "El flamenco no se puede planear, no se deja obligar. Más bien es como una estrella fugaz, a veces como un rayo, que te rasga el corazón". A pesar de eso cada vez se abren más escuelas de flamenco. Tras el taconeo de las botas flamencas se entreven la rabia y el orgullo de un pueblo, mientras que el flexible movimiento de las manos transmite su ternura. Para cuando el tocador empieza a hacer bailar con las yemas las cuerdas de la guitarra, la audiencia ya hace rato que está entregada al singular ritmo del flamenco.
También uno de los indiscutibles bastiones de Andalucía, las corridas de toros, sigue un muy especial ritmo entre el ser humano y el animal. Andalucía es la cuna de la tauromaquia. A los sones de un pasodoble salen a la plaza los toreros vestidos con sus trajes de luces. Ernest Hemingway describe en "Muerte en la tarde" el miedo y el respeto del torero ante la bestia de 500 kilos y la lúdica ligereza de la estocada mortal. La inteligencia y la habilidad del ser hu-

i motivi di sorpresa e divertimento o come si è svolta l'ultima Semana Santa.
In qualsiasi località dell'Andalusia si tengono le processioni tradizionali della Settimana Santa (Semana Santa). Statue di grandi dimensioni raffiguranti il Salvatore e la Vergine Maria sono trasportate a passo lento, de Paso, dalla folla raccolta in preghiera. Le processioni sono condotte da penitenti che, con ceri e il volto coperto da cappucci a punta, in chiesa benedicono una Madonna ritratta in un'espressione amorevolmente addolorata.
Improvvisamente irrompe un suono deciso che impone il silenzio. La musica si diffonde, incalza. Una voce maschile intona la melodia semplice e senza fine di un lamento, una Saeta, in un canto che ricorda i toni del flamenco.
La canzone richiama un pubblico. Il flamenco non è bello, è la voce dell'anima. Si dice che „il flamenco non si può costruire né forzare. È una scheggia di stella, a volte un lampo che squarcia il cuore." Eppure spuntano sempre più numerose le scuole di flamenco. Dietro lo staccato battuto dai tacchi degli stivali si nascondono rabbia ed orgoglio, i movimenti delle mani esprimono dolcezza. Il Tocador vola con le dita sulle corde della chitarra e già da tempo gli spettatori si sono uniti al suo ritmo.
A quella particolare dialettica tra l'uomo e l'animale soggiace il contestato simbolo dell'Andalusia: la corrida. L'Andalusia è la culla di questa tradizione. Ai suoni del pasodoble i toreri adornati per il combattimento entrano nell'arena. In „Morte nel pomeriggio" Ernest Hemingway descrive la paura e il rispetto reverenziale del torero verso quell'animale da 500 chili e, contemporaneamente, la

Harte Jungs ganz anderer Art arbeiten in der einzigen natürlichen Wüste Europas, in der Wüste von Almeria. Gipsfarbene Bodenwellen aus bröckelndem Gestein, ausgedörrte Flussläufe, krüppelige Tamarisken und sengende Hitze. Ein Ort geschaffen für Westernfilme. Andalusisches Hollywood. Sergio Leones „Spiel mir das Lied vom Tod" wurde hier gedreht. Lawrence von Arabien. Cleopatra. Italo-Western. Und der Schuh des Manitu. Heute pilgern überzeugte Westernfans in die Einöde, um Kulissen unvergessener Filme zu sehen. Beherzte Stuntmen schießen und schlägern, Sheriffs sorgen für Recht und Ordnung. Grob gezimmerte Holzhäuser, Saloons, staubige Straßen, der Knast, ein Galgen halten das Flair am Leben. Das Flair Amerikas.

Dagegen herrscht englisches Flair in Gibraltar. Rote Telefonzellen, dunkle Pubs, englisches Bier. Gibraltar, am Südzipfel Europas befindet sich auf spanischem Boden, ist aber britisches Territorium. Das hängt mit dem Friedensschluss von Utrecht im Jahr 1713 zusammen. Heute existieren auf Gibraltar vor allem Briefkastenfirmen und Shopping-Schnäppchen. Und auf dem 425 Meter hohen Felsen springen, betteln und beißen Europas einzige freilebende Affen. Kontrast pur. So kontrastreich wie ganz Andalusien.

and skill of the man must overcome the brute force of the beast, or so say the ancient rules of bullfighting.

Tough guys of quite a different type work in the only natural desert in Europe, the desert of Almeria. Gypsum-coloured undulating terrain of crumbling rock, dried up river beds, misshapen tamarisks and scorching heat. A location just made for western films. The Hollywood of Andalusia. Sergio Leone's "Once Upon a Time in the West" was made here, as was "Lawrence of Arabia", "Cleopatra", and many other spaghetti westerns. Today, dedicated fans of westerns make the pilgrimage to the desert to see the settings of unforgettable films. Plucky stuntmen stage gunfights, while sheriffs try to keep law and order. Rough timbered houses, saloons, dusty streets, the jailhouse and a gallows keep the atmosphere alive – the atmosphere of the Wild West.

A completely English atmosphere however can be found not far away in Gibraltar. Red telephone booths, dark pubs, English beer. Lying at the southern tip of Europe, Gibraltar is on Spanish soil, although it is British territory. This stems from the Treaty of Utrecht concluded in the year 1713. Today, Gibraltar serves mainly as the accommodation address of letter-box companies and a place to find shopping bargains, while on the 1,400 ft. high Rock of Gibraltar, Europe's only free-living "apes" – actually Barbary macaques – leap around begging for food and occasionally biting the unwary visitor. Pure contrast, as contrasting as the rest of Andalusia.

térisé par des ondulations de terrain formées de roches friables couleur de gypse, des cours d'eau asséchés, des tamaris rabougris et une chaleur torride : un décor idéal pour y tourner des westerns. Le Hollywood andalou. C'est ici qu'a été tourné le film « Il était une fois dans l'ouest » de Sergio Leone. Mais aussi Lawrence d'Arabie, Cléopâtre et de nombreux westerns spaghettis. Aujourd'hui, les fans de westerns visitent ce coin perdu pour contempler les décors de films inoubliables. Et le spectacle en vaut la peine : des cascadeurs courageux tirent des coups de feu et se battent pendant que de vaillants shérifs veillent à faire respecter l'ordre et la loi dans un décor qui fait revivre l'ouest américain avec ses maisons en bois rudimentaires, ses saloons, ses rues poussiéreuses, sa prison et sa potence. Une ambiance à l'américaine.

L'ambiance qui règne à Gibraltar en revanche est très anglaise. Des cabines téléphoniques rouges, des pubs sombres, de la bière anglaise ... Gibraltar, à la pointe sud de l'Europe, se trouve certes sur le sol espagnol mais en territoire britannique suite au Traité de Paix d'Utrecht signé en 1713. Aujourd'hui, Gibraltar est surtout le paradis des sociétés fantômes et du commerce de produits bon marché. Et sur le rocher de 425 m de haut, on peut voir sauter, mendier et mordre les seuls singes vivant en liberté en Europe. Encore un contraste incroyable, comme dans toute l'Andalousie.

mano deben vencer sobre la fuerza bruta del toro. Así lo quieren las antiquísimas reglas de la corrida.

En el único desierto natural de Europa, en el desierto de Almería, también muestra su arte tipos duros, pero de una clase muy diferente. Es un panorama caracterizado por ondulaciones del terreno formadas por rocas resquebrajas del color del yeso, cauces secos de torrentes, tamariscos retorcidos y un calor de justicia: un lugar como creado para rodar películas del oeste. Un Hollywood andaluz. Aquí se rodó la película de Sergio Leone "Hasta que llegó su hora". También "Lawrence de Arabia", "Cleopatra" así como numerosas películas de spaghetti western. Hoy en día los aficionados a las películas del oeste peregrinan a estas soledades para contemplar los decorados de sus películas preferidas. Y el espectáculo vale la pena: osados especialistas disparan y se pelean mientras que valientes "sheriffs" se ocupan de restablecer el orden en un escenario que mantiene vivo con sus casas de madera, sus "saloons", sus calles polvorientas, la cárcel y una horca el ambiente del lejano oeste de América.

Por el contrario en Gibraltar reina una atmósfera británica. Cabinas de teléfono rojas, oscuros pubs, cerveza inglesa... Gibraltar, en el extremo sur de Europa, se encuentra sobre suelo español, pero es un territorio británico. El origen de esta situación está en el Tratado de Utrecht de 1713. Hoy Gibraltar sirve sobre todo de base para compañías fantasma y comercios de productos baratos. Y sobre la roca de 425 metros de altura saltan, mendigan e incluso muerden los únicos monos en libertad de Europa. Un tremendo contraste. Como toda Andalucía.

giocosa leggerezza del rituale dell'uccisione del toro. Intelligenza e abilità umane devono trionfare sulla furia brutale taurina, come ha decretato l'antichissima regola della corrida.

Rudi sono anche i personaggi che lavorano nell'unico deserto naturale in Europa, il deserto di Almeria. Paesaggi ondulati color gesso in rocce friabili, greti asciutti di fiumi, tamerici contorte e caldo cocente. Una perfetta scenografia da film western. La Hollywood andalusa. Qui è stato girato „C'era una volta il West" di Sergio Leone. Lawrence d'Arabia. Cleopatra. Gli spaghetti-western e la scarpa di Manitù. Oggi questa landa desolata è meta di grandi appassionati di queste produzioni cinematografiche. Vanno a vedere le scenografie di film indimenticabili. Arditi stuntmen sparano e s'azzuffano, sceriffi riportano la giustizia e l'ordine. Catapecchie in legno, saloons, strade polverose, prigione e forca completano un quadro tipicamente americano.

Britannico è invece l'aplomb di Gibilterra. Le cabine telefoniche rosse, i pubs bui, la birra inglese. Gibilterra, la punta estrema a sud dell'Europa, è terra spagnola ma territorio britannico, come stabilito dal Trattato di Utrecht nel 1713. Oggi a Gibilterra si trovano soprattutto ditte di cassette portalettere e shopping a basso costo. E sulla rupe alta 425 metri saltano, cercano cibo e mordono le ultime scimmie che vivono allo stato brado in Europa. Uno tra i tanti contrasti dell'Andalusia, la terra degli opposti.

1	Puente de Plaza de España, Sevilla
2	Antequera
3	Hacienda a Antequera
4	Berga
5	Almodóvar del Rio
6	Olvera
7	Mezquita de Córdoba
8	Arcos de la Frontera
9	Zahara de la Sierra
10	Antequera
11	Bubión, Sierra Nevada
12	Berga
13	Guadix
14	Mezquita de Córdoba
15	Olvera
16	Zahara de los Atunes
17	Torrox
18	Arcos de la Frontera
19	Guadix
20	Zahara de la Sierra
21 | 22	El Rocio
23	Cádiz
24	Pabellón de la Energía Viva, Sevilla
25	El Rocio
26	Granada
27 | 28 | 29	Alhambra, Granada
30	Catedral, Sevilla
31 | 32	Mezquita de Córdoba
33	Málaga
34	Hacienda a Baena
35 | 36	Jaén
37	Hacienda a Vejer de la Frontera
38	Carmona
39	Alhambra, Granada
40	Puente de la Barqueta, Sevilla
41 | 42 | 43	Alhambra, Granada
44	Teatro Lope de Vega, Sevilla
45	Plaza de Toros, Sevilla
46 | 47	Santa María de las Cuevas (Monasterio de la Cartuja), Sevilla
48	Plaza de España, Sevilla
49	Giralda, Sevilla
50	Monumento a la Tolerancia Eduardo Chillida, Sevilla

5
7
14
31
32
34
35
36
1
24
30
40
44
45
46
47
48
49
50
38
21
22
25
2
3
10
26
28
27
39
29
43
41
42
13
19
11
6
15
4
12
9
20
17
33
8
18
23
37
16

1 Puente de Plaza de España, Sevilla

2 Antequera

► 3 Hacienda a Antequera

5 Almodóvar del Rio

7 Mezquita de Córdoba

 Arcos de la Frontera

► 9 Zahara de la Sierra

11 Bubión, Sierra Nevada

12 Berga

13 Guadix

► 15 Olvera

17 Torrox

► **19** Guadix

 Zahara de la Sierra

21 El Rocio

AVE MARIA
CASA HERMANDAD DE LOS PALACIOS

23 Cádiz

TE AMO MAS

 Pabellón de la Energía Viva, Sevilla

► 25 El Rocio

HERMANDAD DE VALVERDE
1935

► 27 Alhambra, Granada

28 Alhambra, Granada

29 Alhambra, Granada

30 Catedral, Sevilla

31 Mezquita de Córdoba

► **32** Mezquita de Córdoba

33 Málaga

 Hacienda a Baena

35 Jaén

37 Hacienda a Vejer de la Frontera

39 Alhambra, Granada

40 Puente de la Barqueta, Sevilla

► **41** Alhambra, Granada

42 Alhambra, Granada

► 43 Alhambra, Granada

44 Teatro Lope de Vega, Sevilla

TEATRO LOPE DE VEGA

45 Plaza de Toros, Sevilla

TAQUILLAS
TAQUILLAS

46 Santa María de las Cuevas (Monasterio de la Cartuja), Sevilla

47 Santa María de las Cuevas (Monasterio de la Cartuja), Sevilla

► **48** Plaza de España, Sevilla

49 Giralda, Sevilla

► **50** Monumento a la Tolerancia Eduardo Chillida, Sevilla

POR LA TOLERANCIA.

KARL LANG wurde 1932 in Duisburg geboren. Nach der Ausbildung zum Industrie- und Werbephotograph arbeitete er für verschiedene Bildagenturen. Von 1965 bis 1993 leitete er die Photoabteilung der Thyssen Unternehmensgruppe. 1985 gründete er das eigene Photostudio in Essen, das sich auf Industriephotographie spezialisierte. Seine Reisen führten ihn auf alle Kontinente dieser Erde, seine Aufnahmen wurden vielfach ausgestellt und u. a. in Turin, Hongkong, Newcastle, Fribourg und Johannesburg prämiert. Karl Lang wurde im Jahr 2000 für seine Photoserie „Bridges“ mit dem renommierten World Press Photo Award ausgezeichnet.

IRIS LEMANCZYK wurde 1964 in Kirchheim/Teck bei Stuttgart geboren. Nach dem Studium der Germanistik und Geographie lockte immer wieder die Ferne. Sie reiste um die Welt, schnupperte eine Zeit lang Zirkusluft, lebte in Namibia und besuchte für ein paar Monate Australien und Neuseeland. Dazwischen arbeitete sie als Zeitungs-Redakteurin bei der „Südwest Presse“ in Ulm. Seit 1997 ist sie freiberuflich tätig, schreibt Kinder- und Jugendbücher sowie Sachbücher, verfasst Reiseberichte und ist als Dozentin für Kreatives Schreiben tätig.

KARL LANG was born in 1932 in Duisburg. After his training as industrial and commercial photographer he worked for several Photo Agencies. From 1965 to 1993 he was head of the photo department of the Thyssen group. In 1985 he established his own photo studio in Essen, which specialized in industrial photography. He travelled widely on all continents of the earth and his images were exhibited many times and at many places such as Turin, Hong Kong, Newcastle, Fribourg and Johannesburg, where they also received awards. For his photo series “Bridges”, Karl Lang received the renowned World Press Photo Award in the year 2000.

IRIS LEMANCZYK was born in 1964 in Kirchheim/Teck near Stuttgart. After studying German and geography, she gave way to the call of far-distant places. She travelled around the world, experienced the circus life for a time, lived in Namibia and spent several months in Australia and New Zealand. In between, she also learnt something more conventional: newspaper editing with the “Südwest Presse” in Ulm. Since 1997 she has worked as a freelancer, writing children’s books and non-fiction and compiling travel reports, and also works as a lecturer on creative writing.

KARL LANG est né en 1932 à Duisbourg. Après une formation de photographe industriel et publicitaire, il travaille pour différentes agences. De 1965 à 1993, il dirige le service de photographie du groupe d'entreprises Thyssen. Il fonde en 1985 son propre studio de photographie à Essen, qui se spécialise dans la photographie industrielle. Ses voyages le menent sur tous les continents, ses travaux sont exposés à de nombreuses reprises et notamment primés à Turin, Hongkong, Newcastle, Fribourg et Johannesburg. Karl Lang obtient en 2000 pour sa série de photographies « Bridges » la célèbre distinction World Press Photo Award.

IRIS LEMANCZYK est née en 1964 à Kirchheim/Teck près de Stuttgart. Après des études de philologie allemande et de géographie, elle effectue régulièrement des voyages lointains. Elle voyage à travers le monde, séjourne pendant quelque temps dans un cirque, vit en Namibie et passe plusieurs mois en Australie et en Nouvelle-Zélande. Entre toutes ces occupations, elle trouve néanmoins le temps d'apprendre un métier sérieux : rédactrice journalistique au quotidien allemand « Südwest Presse » à Ulm. Depuis 1997, elle travaille comme rédactrice indépendante, écrit des livres destinés à l'enfance et à la jeunesse ainsi que des livres d'essai. Elle rédige également des comptes rendus de voyage et dispense des cours de création littéraire.

KARL LANG nació en 1932 en Duisburg (Alemania). Tras concluir su formación de fotógrafo publicitario e industrial trabajó para diversas agencias de fotografía. Entre 1965 y 1993 dirigió el departamento de fotografía del consorcio empresarial Thyssen. En 1985 fundó su propio estudio dedicado a la fotografía industrial en Essen. Él ha celebrado varias exposiciones dedicadas a las fotografías que ha realizado durante sus viajes por todos los continentes. Sus obras han sido premiadas en diversos eventos realizados en Turín, Hongkong, Newcastle, Friburgo y Johannesburgo. En 2000 Karl Lang fue galardonado con el prestigioso premio "World Press Photo Award" por su serie fotográfica "Bridges".

IRIS LEMANCZYK nació en 1964 en el pueblo de Kirchheim/Teck junto a Stuttgart (Alemania). Tras terminar su carrera de Filología Germánica y Geografía se dejó atraer cada vez más por el encanto de los destinos exóticos: viajó por el mundo, experimentó durante algún tiempo la vida en un circo, residió en Namibia y pasó algunos meses en Australia y Nueva Zelanda. Y entre todas esas ocupaciones todavía encontró tiempo para aprender un oficio serio: redactora de periódicos en la editorial alemana "Südwest Presse" de Ulm. Desde 1997 trabaja como redactora libre y escribe diversos libros: desde literatura infantil y juvenil a libros de texto. Además confecciona relatos de viaje e imparte seminarios de creación literaria.

KARL LANG è nato nel 1932 a Duisburg. Dopo un corso di formazione a fotografo industriale e pubblicitario lavorò per diverse agenzie fotografiche. Dal 1965 al 1993 egli diresse il reparto di fotografia del Gruppo imprenditoriale Thyssen. Nel 1985 fondò il proprio studio fotografico a Essen, specializzandosi in fotografia industriale. I suoi viaggi lo hanno portato in tutti i continenti di questo pianeta, le sue immagini sono state esposte in molte località e premiate tra l'altro a Torino, Hongkong, Newcastle, Fribourg e Johannesburg. Nel 2000 è stato conferito a Karl Lang per la sue serie di fotografie "Bridges" il rinomato World Press Photo Award.

IRIS LEMANCZYK è nata nel 1964 a Kirchheim/Teck vicino a Stoccarda. Dopo la laurea in Lingua e Letteratura Tedesca e in Geografia ha seguito la sua passione per i viaggi in paesi lontani. È stata in tutto il mondo, per un certo periodo ha respirato l'aria del circo, ha vissuto in Namibia e per qualche mese ha abitato in Australia e Nuova Zelanda. Tra un viaggio e l'altro si è dedicata alla più razionale attività di redattrice presso la Südwest Presse di Ulm. Dal 1997 lavora come libera professionista, scrive libri per bambini e ragazzi e testi di saggistica, redige reportage di viaggi ed insegna scrittura creativa.

ISBN: 978-3-89823-333-0

Concept: Bernhard Wipfler, Sebastian Wipfler, Marcus Bela Schmitt
Design: EDITION PANORAMA | Diana May and Designgruppe Fanz & Neumayer | Marcus Bela Schmitt
Editorial department: Dr. Michael Barchet, Wolfgang Roth
Translations: Global-Text Fachübersetzungen, Heidelberg | Mark Woolfe, Jocelyne Abarca, Dr. Maria Carasi, Sebastián González Mohíno
Separations: EPS GmbH, Speyer
Printing: abcdruck GmbH, Heidelberg
Bookbinding: Josef Spinner Großbuchbinderei GmbH, Ottersweier

EDITION PANORAMA GmbH
G7, 14
D - 68159 Mannheim

www.editionpanorama.com

A production by EDITION**PANORAMA**